Let's Get Moving™

The HOPPING Book

Jennifer Way

The Rosen Publishing Group's
PowerStart Press™
New York

1

For Mike—Hopalong, get on the good foot!

Published in 2004 by The Rosen Publishing Group, Inc.
29 East 21st Street, New York, NY 10010

First Edition

Book Design: Maria E. Melendez
Developmental Editor: Nancy Allison, Certified Movement Analyst, Registered Movement Educator

Photo Credits: All photos by Maura B. McConnell.

Library of Congress Cataloging-in-Publication Data

Way, Jennifer.
The hopping book / Jennifer Way.— 1st ed.
    p. cm. — (Let's get moving)
Includes index.
Summary: Pictures and brief captions describe the movements involved in hopping.
ISBN 1-4042-2514-5 (lib. bdg.)
1. Jumping—Juvenile literature. [1. Jumping.] I. Title. II. Series.
QP310.J86 W39 2004
573.7'9—dc21
                                        2003006030

Manufactured in the United States of America

Contents

I hop.

I hop high.

I hop on my right foot.

9

I hop on my left foot.

11

I hop to the side.

13

I hop
over the
line.

15

I hop a big hop.

I hop a small hop.

I hop and
hop and
hop!

21

I like to hop.

23

Words to Know

hop

left

right

side

Index

Web Sites

Due to the changing nature of Internet links, PowerStart Press has developed an online list of Web sites related to the subject of this book. This site is updated regularly. Please use this link to access the list:

www.powerkidslinks.com/lgmov/hop/